The "F

MAN OF PEACE

THE STORY OF MAHATMA GANDHI

Audrey Constant

RMEP

RELIGIOUS AND MORAL EDUCATION PRESS

Religious and Moral Education Press
An imprint of Chansitor Publications Ltd
A Subsidiary Company of Hymns Ancient & Modern Ltd
St Mary's Works, St Mary's Plain
Norwich, Norfolk NR3 3BH

Photographs are reproduced by kind permission of BBC Hulton Picture Library (p. 23), The British Library (p. 19), the High Commission of India (pp. 4, 9, 12) and Keystone Press (p. 25). Cover picture courtesy of The British Library.

First published 1985

New imprint 1991

Reprinted 1992, 1993, 1994

Printed in Great Britain by BPC Wheatons Ltd, Exeter

ISBN 0 900274 46 8 *non net*

MAN OF PEACE

The Story of Mahatma Gandhi

On 31 January 1948 thousands of Indians were waiting under the fierce sun by the banks of the holy river Jumna, near New Delhi. Slowly a procession made its way towards the cremation ground, where a funeral pyre had been built of brick and earth and piled with wood. On it rested the body of Mahatma Gandhi. As the crowds watched, Ramdas, Gandhi's third son, stepped forward and set the pyre alight. The flames leaped and the smell of incense filled the air. The people wailed with grief as the raging fire burnt the body to ashes.

The day before, the Mahatma had died at the hands of an assassin. With his passing had gone not only the father of India but one of the most influential men in history. Gandhi was mourned by people of all races and religions. He moved among the leaders of the world, yet his concern was for the poor and oppressed of his own country.

Gandhi believed that the doctrine of love operating through non-violence is the most powerful weapon available to men. With it he tried to unite India and throw off British rule, which had been maintained in India for more than 150 years.

His country

India is a vast country made up of many provinces and states, many with their own language and traditions. The characteristics of her people and the geography vary too, some states being fertile and their people prosperous while others suffer from drought and people die of disease and famine. In addition, the people follow a number of different religions, Hinduism, Islam, Sikhism, Buddhism and Christianity being the main ones.

In the middle of the nineteenth century India was the most important part of the British Empire and a very difficult region to administer. The larger provinces were ruled by officials appointed by the British Crown and the smaller states were ruled by their own princes, who had limited powers. The British Empire had grown slowly over the years but Britain formally took charge of all India in 1858 when the Indian army mutinied. (At that time India included the areas that in 1948 became East and West Pakistan.)

Although the men who were sent out from England to govern India were not always popular, they did maintain peace and order and brought with them new, European methods. They encouraged more efficient ways of farming and introduced modern industry and communications. Many Indians became prosperous. Under firm government, India had become one country rather than many separate states.

Early years

Mohandas Karamchand Gandhi was born on 2 October 1869 in the little state of Porbandar, on the west coast of India. His father, Karamchand Gandhi, was *dewan* or prime minister of Porbandar. Mohandas, the youngest of three brothers and a sister, was brought up in the family's large ancestral home.

The Gandhis were orthodox Hindus. The Hindu religion has many gods and goddesses, each representing different aspects of one divine power. Mohandas was brought up in the sect of Vishnu, the Preserver of the Universe, and believed in a loving relationship between God and mankind. Mohandas' mother was very religious and he always thought of her as a good, saintly woman who spent a lot of time praying and fasting.

The Hindu caste system divides people into social groups of high and low rank. Originally there were four principal castes: *Brahmins*, the highest caste, who were priests and scholars; *Kshatriyas*, who traditionally were warriors; *Vaisyas* (the caste to which the Gandhis belonged), who were merchants and farmers, and *Sudras*, the craftsmen and peasants. In the course of time these have split into many sub-castes.

There are also outcastes, or Untouchables, people without caste, who are regarded as inferior to members of all castes. Until recently, Untouchables were allowed to do only menial work, such as disposing of excrement, dead animals and human corpses.

Hindus believe that when someone dies they are born again, or reincarnated, and that the caste they are born into depends on their conduct in their previous incarnations. Good behaviour in this life brings promotion in the next.

The name Gandhi means "grocer", but Karamchand Gandhi did not follow this trade. Although the Gandhi family were not distinguished in the caste system they were in fact quite wealthy and owned land and property.

Mohandas was a less-than-average student, self-conscious and serious and deeply devoted to his parents. "My books and lessons were my sole companions," he recalled later. He was so shy that each day he arrived at the

Mohandas Gandhi (right) with his elder brother Laxmidas in 1886

school just on time and ran back home as soon as the classes ended. He could not bear to talk to anyone and was afraid that people would poke fun at him.

He described himself as a coward: "I used to be haunted by the fear of thieves, ghosts and serpents. I did not dare to stir out of doors at night. Darkness was a terror to me."

As he grew older, he got into mischief like other boys. He used to smoke in secret, but felt deeply ashamed of deceiving his parents. His dedication to truth and honesty would never allow Mohandas to lie and once, when he stole some money, he could not rest until he had confessed to his father.

Marriage

When he was thirteen and still at school, Mohandas was married to Kasturbai, a girl who was the same age as himself. Their parents had made the match years before but the children were not told about it until the wedding preparations were complete.

Marriage among Hindus is a costly matter and often brings families to financial ruin. Mohandas' elder brother was already married, so to reduce the cost, the family arranged for the marriage of his second brother and a cousin at the same time.

Kasturbai had no education but she was an attractive girl and Mohandas was passionately fond of her. However, they were quite unprepared for marriage at such an early age and were nervous and unsure of how to behave towards each other. Later Mohandas denounced the "cruel system of child marriages", though at the time he quite enjoyed the preparations and excitement.

Mohandas quickly became an exacting husband. Both the children were strong-willed and the marriage was stormy at the start. Mohandas would not let Kasturbai go out without his permission, and when she asked if she could go and play in the street he would often say no because he was jealous of her. But she was headstrong and made a point of going out when and where she liked. They quarrelled frequently.

It was customary for young brides to return to their parents' home for long periods each year and the boys had to continue their studies at school, so soon Mohandas and Kasturbai were separated for a while.

Mohandas was small, and he longed to be tall and strong. A Muslim friend of his who was good at athletics and afraid of nothing told Mohandas he was brave because he ate meat. Mohandas had often heard the boys at school reciting a rhyme which went:

> Behold the mighty Englishman,
> He rules the Indian small,
> Because being a meat-eater
> He is five cubits tall.

Mohandas never ate meat. His family, like many orthodox Hindus, was strictly vegetarian. Now, urged by his friend, he succumbed to temptation and tried to eat some cooked goat's flesh. It was tough, unpleasant and difficult to swallow and he was immediately sick. He persevered for a while and then gave it up.

In 1885 his father died after a long illness through which Mohandas helped to nurse him. Gradually the family fortunes had declined and little property was left. It was important that Mohandas should qualify for a profession. In 1887 he managed to scrape through his high-school examination. Then a family friend suggested that he should go to England for three years to study law.

Mohandas welcomed the suggestion, but how was the money to be found? He also came up against opposition from leaders of his caste community. They forbade him to go to England, where, they said, he would be exposed to temptation to eat and drink with Europeans. He overcame this problem by making a solemn vow before his mother to abstain from wine, women and meat. Then Kasturbai, who had now borne him a son, sold her jewellery to buy his ticket. Sadly parting from her, he sailed for England on 4 September, 1888.

Studies in England

Gandhi was not yet nineteen when he landed in England. Shy and self-conscious as he was, the first few months seemed a nightmare. He spoke hardly any English and everything around him was different. He was desperately homesick and often on the verge of taking the next boat home, but his pride would not allow it. He forced himself to settle down and study law.

He was often hungry because it was difficult to find the

kind of food he could eat. Nearly everything contained meat or eggs and other food was unappetising after the rich spices of Indian cooking. English and Indian friends tried to persuade him that meat was essential for good health, but Gandhi would not break his promise. Then one day he found a vegetarian restaurant which led to him joining a vegetarian society.

Gandhi copied the well-dressed young men about town and enjoyed buying new clothes. He took dancing lessons, at which he was hopeless, followed by violin and elocution lessons.

Soon he realised that this way of living was beyond the modest means of his family. He cut down his expenses by giving up frivolous pastimes, moving into cheaper accommodation and cooking most of his own meals.

It was while he was in London that some friends asked him to read the Bhagavad-gita with them. This sacred book of the Hindus is in the form of a poem. Although Gandhi had often seen it at home, he had never read it before and now it struck him as a book of priceless worth. One passage made a deep impression on him: "The man who forsakes all desires and puts aside all pride of possession and pride in himself reaches the goal of supreme peace." In later life he studied every word of the Bhagavad-gita and learned it by heart.

After this he went on to study the Bible. The Sermon on the Mount (Matthew, chapters 5-7) affected him deeply and he carried the words of Jesus in his heart throughout his life.

On 10 June 1891 he passed his law examinations and was enrolled as a barrister at the Inner Temple, one of the Inns of Court in London. The next day he sailed for Bombay. His elder brother Laxmidas met him with the sad news of his mother's death, which they had kept from him during his exams.

Finding work

When Gandhi joined his family in Rajkot they had high hopes that, with his qualifications, he would soon build up a successful law practice. But there were already too many lawyers in Rajkot. Besides, in spite of passing his exams he had little knowledge of how to apply his English book-learning to situations in India.

While in England Gandhi had become used to western ideas and now he tried to impose them on his family. He insisted that Kasturbai, who had grown into a beautiful young woman, should learn to read and write. As strong-willed as ever, she would not be changed.

In order to gain experience in the High Court Gandhi went to Bombay. He was given a court case to handle but was so tongue-tied with nervousness that he had to abandon it and give his client back his money. Disheartened by failure, he returned to Rajkot, not knowing what to try next.

Then a Muslim merchant from Porbandar who had business connections in South Africa offered him a year's contract to undertake some legal work in Durban. He offered Gandhi £105 and all living and travelling expenses. Even though it meant again leaving Kasturbai, who now had another baby son, Gandhi accepted the job. He gave the money to Laxmidas and asked him to look after his family while he was away. He left for Durban in May 1893.

South Africa

Indians had first come to South Africa in 1860, to work on the sugar plantations of Natal. By 1893 there were large Indian communities in Natal and the Transvaal. Europeans in South Africa saw these communities as a political threat. They made it very difficult for Indians to enter the country and made it almost impossible for those already there to

Gandhi and his wife Kasturbai

obtain trading licences. Racial discrimination was rife and Indians, along with black Africans, were held to be second-class citizens.

It was not long before Gandhi experienced this for himself. One day he had to go to Pretoria. Although he had a first-class train ticket, he was told to move to a third-class compartment. When he refused, he was thrown out on to the platform. All night, angry and shivering with cold, he struggled to understand this injustice. It was not his own humiliation and injuries that infuriated him but the persecution of people for differences in colour or belief.

That night he decided to stay in South Africa and try to improve conditions for Indians living there. He planned to use an entirely new method of fighting. He believed that wrongdoing could be overcome simply by returning love for hatred and respect for contempt, refusing to yield to injustice. He invented a name for the two weapons he would use: *satyagraha* (holding on to truth), which meant standing up for something you were convinced was right, and *ahimsa*, meaning love operating through non-violence.

For the next twenty years Gandhi rallied Indians and fought to obtain equal rights for them. It was a long struggle that sometimes landed him in prison.

In 1896 he brought his family to live in South Africa.

At this time Gandhi's search for religious faith became more earnest and he had long discussions with Christians and Muslims. It seemed to him that there was some truth in most religions. There was much about Hinduism he disliked, such as the glitter and pomp of the temples, and the animal sacrifices. He visited a Christian missionary community in Zululand and was impressed by the atmosphere of peace. He thought that one day he would found such a community himself.

He felt that if he was to follow God, he must give up his

possessions and suffer for his people. He simplified his way of life and expected his family to do the same. Kasturbai had to sell her jewels and work as she had never worked at home. Gandhi refused to let any of his sons have a proper education. He intended to supervise their education himself, but he seldom had time to do it properly. Although Kasturbai protested, she usually gave way to his wishes.

In 1899 war broke out between Britain and the two Boer republics, the Transvaal and the Orange Free State (the Boers were South Africans of Dutch descent). Gandhi encouraged Indians to demonstrate their loyalty to the Government by forming a corps of stretcher-bearers in which he himself served.

In spite of their loyalty to Britain, Indians continued to be treated as inferiors, so Gandhi continued to fight for their rights. He proved himself an excellent organiser and an effective leader. He won the support of many influential men who were impressed by his arguments and the force of his honesty. Eventually, as a result of his talks with General Smuts, the South African Minister of Defence, many of the regulations against Indians were abolished.

Gandhi in India

Gandhi returned to India in 1915. He was now recognised as a national figure and, owing to his teaching on non-violence, had gained a reputation as a spiritual leader. Rabindranath Tagore, one of India's greatest writers, called Gandhi "a great soul in peasant's garb" and so the title Mahatma (Great Soul) was conferred on him. But Gandhi disliked any honour which put him above the ordinary people of India. He once told Tagore: "The suffering millions need only one poem – food."

During the first year of his return he avoided making any

comments on the political situation in India, but he did travel widely over the country looking into social problems. He believed that if India was to achieve independence, Indians themselves must change. He tried to persuade them to give up their superstitions and their intolerance of castes other than their own and to live according to the principles in their holy book, the Bhagavad-gita.

Over eighty per cent of India's population lived in her villages and were illiterate and in poor health. Gandhi felt that, in order for conditions to improve, these people must be properly educated. He began by opening six primary schools. Volunteer teachers were to be supported by the villagers, who gave them food and accommodation. Gandhi told the teachers to concentrate less on grammar and arithmetic and more on cleanliness and good manners.

Britain exported huge quantities of cotton cloth to India. Gandhi believed that developing Indian village industries

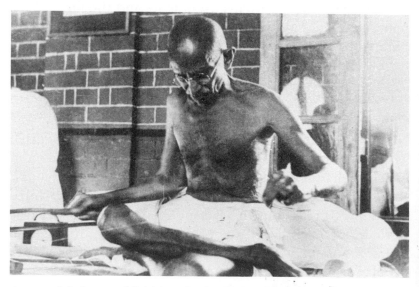

As part of the boycott of British goods, Gandhi urged Indians to spin their own cloth. He also recommended spinning as a form of relaxation

and boycotting foreign cloth would bring India a step nearer independence. He introduced a policy of *Swadeshi* (of the country) and designed a simple spinning-wheel with which *khaddar*, homespun cloth, could be produced.

Gandhi's next step was to found an *ashram* or religious retreat in Ahmadabad. His followers led a life of prayer, study, manual work and helping local people. Every day they had to do some spinning, which Gandhi believed relaxed the mind. The community lived in a group of small whitewashed huts in a grove of shady trees near the river. The Mahatma himself lived in a small cell. He spent his time praying, and teaching anyone who came. Among the members of the community were some of India's most influential leaders. Gandhi lived at the ashram on and off for sixteen years, keeping in close touch with the outside world.

Satyagraha and ahimsa
In 1914 the First World War had broken out. However much he criticised the Government, the Mahatma saw himself as a loyal subject of the Crown and urged the people to fight for the Empire. While Indian soldiers fought in Europe and the Middle East, Gandhi was occupied with troubles at home. His attention was drawn to many cases where peasants were unjustly treated and to these he applied his weapons of satyagraha and ahimsa.

He taught his followers that satyagraha springs from an inner conviction of truth and justice. It must never be used as a result of anger. He explained that ahisma (non-violence) does not mean weak submission; it is the capacity to love those who hate you, to show patience and understanding in the face of the fiercest opposition.

One day a farmer asked Gandhi to visit Champaran, where peasants were burdened by the high rents and taxes their landlords demanded. When the Government made no response to Gandhi's protest, he organised a strike. He made four rules: 1. Never resort to violence; 2. Never molest non-strikers; 3. Never beg for food; 4. Never give in. He believed they could win if they obeyed these rules faithfully.

When the landlords responded with violence, the strikers stood firm and did not fight back. At last a commission gave Gandhi's arguments a hearing and acted upon them. The landlords were ordered to repay what they had unjustly taken from their tenants.

The Mahatma went on to settle more disputes, sometimes fasting to win better conditions for the workers.

Amritsar

When Britain won the war in 1918 Gandhi and other Indian leaders hoped there would be a movement towards self-rule, but they were to be disappointed. The British Government sent a delegation to study the political situation in India. In March 1919 an Act was passed that, far from preparing India for self-rule, imposed measures to discourage any move towards independence.

Indian leaders felt deceived and betrayed. On 6 April 1919 Gandhi launched a *hartal* or general strike throughout the country. The people fasted to show the Government that they would not accept the new laws. Shops were shut and factories stood idle.

The hartal was intended to demonstrate the people's unity and strength, but it failed. Feelings were running so high that Gandhi's rules for non-violence were forgotten. Many people were injured in the fighting. Realising that things had got out of hand, Gandhi called off the hartal. He knew it had been a disastrous mistake to call for civil disobedience before the people were ready for it.

Worse was to come. Many Punjabi soldiers had served loyally in the war and in the Sikhs' holy city of Amritsar there was discontent. For fear of open revolt, the army was called in and all meetings were banned. August 12 was a religious festival and large crowds in holiday mood gathered in a square for the celebrations. They were listening to a speaker when General Dyer's troops opened fire on them. Panic broke out as people struggled to escape, and hundreds of people died.

India was stunned. Martial law was declared in Amritsar and leading Sikhs were thrown into jail. Gandhi's request to visit the city was refused. He looked with horror at the British Empire in which he had had so much faith.

For the rest of his life the Mahatma observed a twenty-four-hour fast on the anniversary of the Amritsar massacre.

National leader

After the Amritsar massacre the Government promised reforms, but when, a year later, little had changed, Gandhi relaunched his policy of non-co-operation. He was now leader of the Indian National Congress, the most important political party in India. The people trusted him and he had the support of Muslims and Hindus, among them many politicians. One of them was Jawaharlal Nehru, an influential lawyer and devoted friend of Gandhi's.

As part of the campaign, Government institutions and British goods were boycotted, many schools and universities were closed and peasants refused to pay their taxes.

For seven months Gandhi himself toured the countryside preaching in support of his programme of non-violent civil disobedience. He travelled in packed, hot trains and addressed huge crowds wherever he went. Tens of thousands of people flocked to catch a glimpse of the

Mahatma, who in their eyes was holy. At small stations where the train was not due to halt, people would lie down on the tracks to stop it.

There were extremists who thought that Britain could be driven from India, but Gandhi would never agree to independence won by force. He hoped that if he could contain India's anger by demonstrating peacefully Britain would give in. An incident in which twenty-two policemen were murdered brought the campaign to a close. Gandhi was no longer sure he could control the angry crowds. He said: "It is better to be charged with cowardice and weakness than to sin against God by denying our oath of non-violence."

In March 1922 he was arrested and accused of persuading others to disobey the law. He was sentenced to six years' imprisonment. In prison, he spent much of his time praying, writing and spinning.

After two years he became very ill. He was released and a British surgeon operated on him for appendicitis. The operation was successful but recovery was slow. Two Muslim doctors looked after him as he slowly improved. During this time he wrote articles about the need for unity between Hindus and Muslims. "Before they think of freedom," he wrote, "they must be brave enough to love one another."

He knew that it was important for India to solve the problem of the division between the two religious groups. For many years Hindus and Muslims had lived peacefully together in Indian villages and in the army they fought side by side. It was not until the twentieth century, when people crowded into cities to look for work, that trouble began. Riots often started with small incidents, such as a Hindu religious procession passing by a Muslim mosque at prayer-time. The Hindus, who regard the cow as holy, became angry when Muslims killed and ate cattle. There was rivalry for jobs, too. The rioting and turmoil spread.

When Gandhi heard there had been a clash between the Hindu and Muslim communities in the North-East Frontier province, although he was not yet fully recovered, he started a three-week fast. Only when he was almost at the point of death did Hindu and Muslim leaders all over India urge their followers to live in peace.

The Salt March

In December 1928 India was seething with unrest. Ten years of bitter repression had passed since Gandhi had launched his policy of non-co-operation, and Britain had merely tightened her hold on India. Gandhi went to London to try to find a solution, but without success. In 1929 the Indian National Congress party voted in favour of complete independence and withdrawal from the Empire.

The tension increased. Everyone looked to Gandhi to see what would happen next. Even he did not seem to know what to do. After weeks of prayer and deliberation, the answer came to him in a dream. It was simple: the Government had imposed a law forbidding Indians to make their own salt, forcing them to depend on a Government supply. He would use this to bring India's troubles to the attention of the world.

On 12 March 1930, with eighty disciples from his ashram, the Mahatma made the long march to the sea. It took twenty-four days. Thousands joined the marching column on the way.

When they arrived at the seashore they prayed throughout the night for strength to resist the violence which could easily have swept the crowd. At dawn they went quietly down to the water, where Gandhi stooped and picked up a pinch of salt from the sand. Following his example, peasants all along India's coastline immediately waded into the water with pans and illegally produced salt, which they later sold to the cities. The police made many arrests but there was no hint of trouble from the people.

Gandhi, Nehru and thousands of others were sent to prison for infringing the Salt Act but hope was high. It was not long before the manufacture of salt was permitted and political prisoners were freed.

Visit to London

In 1931, while he was still in prison, Gandhi received an invitation to attend a conference in London as the representative of India's Congress party.

As Gandhi was a guest of the Crown, very comfortable accommodation had been arranged for him, but he turned it down in favour of a modest hotel in a poorer part of London.

Although little came of the Round Table Conference, as it

The 1931 Round Table Conference at India House, London

was known, Gandhi stayed on in London for three months, talking to political leaders and visiting ordinary British people in their homes. Often he spoke at public meetings about what he wanted for India.

He was invited to Buckingham Palace to have tea with George V and Queen Mary. As usual he wore his peasant's clothes, sandals and a shawl. When a shocked reporter enquired about his dress, Gandhi replied with a smile, "The King will be wearing enough for both of us."

While in England, Gandhi made a point of visiting Lancashire, where most of the textile mills were. Under British rule India had to export all its cotton to England at a low price. The cotton was manufactured into cloth and sold back to India at a high profit. When Gandhi had encouraged Indians to spin their own cloth, British textile workers had been thrown out of work. Understandably, the unemployed millhands Gandhi met in Lancashire were angry and resentful of him at first. He spoke to them quietly, pleading the cause of the people of India, who were far worse off than they were. Gradually the mood changed and before he left they were cheering him.

The people of Lancashire understood Gandhi, but the British Government did not. Britain wanted to maintain control of India. On his return, the Mahatma found that a new Viceroy had been installed, a man who believed that a firm hand would defeat Congress. Thirty-five thousand people were arrested and once again Gandhi was imprisoned, along with other political leaders.

The children of God
Gandhi believed in the equality of all men, including the tens of millions of Untouchables who were outcastes, forced to live in slums. High-caste Hindus believed themselves

polluted if the Untouchables used the same wells, entered their temples, or even if an Untouchable's shadow fell across them.

Gandhi called them *Harijans* (God's children) and devoted himself to giving them self-respect. When an Untouchable family wanted to join his ashram the Mahatma accepted them, but with dire consequences. Wealthy caste Hindus stopped giving the ashram financial help and others threatened to boycott the ashram and drive its members away, but there were other Hindus who continued to support it.

Gandhi was against the principle of separating Harijans from the main community of Hindus, so emphasising their differences. But at a conference held in 1932 Britain had given Untouchables separate political representation. Gandhi protested by fasting, this time not against the British but to shake the rigid attitude of caste Hindus. "What I want," he said, "what I am living for and what I should be pleased to die for is removal of Untouchability, root and branch."

He was not afraid to die, because he knew that the soul never dies, but he had become desperately weak and Kasturbai was moved into Yeravada prison to be with him. Her presence cheered him. When he was very close to death, British officials became alarmed and tried to find a solution. Indian leaders came to see him to try to persuade him to give up the fast, and Hindus all over India said they were prepared to overcome traditional differences and allow Untouchables into their temples.

Eventually an agreement was reached and the Mahatma ended his fast. Harijans now have constitutional rights and some of them reach high positions in business and in government, for example, but in some areas the caste system remains almost unchanged.

Towards independence

When the Second World War broke out in Europe in 1939, Gandhi's sympathies were for Britain and France. If Germany and Japan drove the British out of India, independence would be impossible to achieve without an armed struggle.

In India there was growing opposition to Congress from the Muslim League. The leader of the Muslim League, Ali Jinnah, wanted a separate independent Muslim state, which he planned to call Pakistan. He would not agree to a united India because Muslims, who were in a minority, would be dominated by Hindus, and the Hindus would hold most of the government posts and enjoy other economic advantages. A separate Pakistan would give Muslims political power and control over industry and trade.

Jinnah proposed that Pakistan should be composed of six provinces, three in the west and three in the east, amounting to a quarter of the total area of India. But Gandhi would not consider a divided India. Britain refused to make any concessions until the conflicting groups in India spoke with one voice.

In 1942 Gandhi was again arrested. Although he had retired from active politics some years before, he still had a great deal of influence, and the authorities were worried that he would make trouble by stirring up opposition to the war effort in India. Gandhi condemned Nazism and Fascism, but he was opposed to war or violence of any kind.

He spent most of the war imprisoned in the Aga Khan's palace at Poona. Here, early in 1944, Kasturbai died, her head in her husband's lap. She too had been imprisoned, and while in prison had gathered support from other women for the Mahatma's campaign.

They had been married for over sixty years and Gandhi was heart-broken at her death. It was Kasturbai, he once said, who taught him how to love. By her example she had shown him the way to root out anger, constantly supporting him and bearing with him through his outbursts. Each month after Kasturbai's death Gandhi would hold a memorial service for her.

In February 1944 Gandhi began a fast, which lasted until he was released from prison, a sick man, the following May.

In 1945 the war ended and a Labour Government was elected in Britain. It promised to grant India self-government under a joint Hindu-Muslim council, but Ali Jinnah continued to insist on separate Hindu and Muslim states. The Mahatma was disgusted. From now on Jinnah, not the British, was to be his greatest problem.

In March 1946 the British sent a Mission to prepare for a smooth handover of power. They asked both the Congress party and the Muslim League to help, but the two sides could not agree, so the Mission had to draft its own programme.

Gandhi urged Congress to accept the Mission's plan. "This is the best document the British Government can produce in the circumstances and it shows firm resolve to end British rule as soon as possible," he told them. However, afraid that the plan would not prevent the division of India, Congress refused to accept it. Nor would Jinnah accept; he pressed on with his claim for a separate Pakistan.

Partition

Then the Mahatma heard that Muslims in the Noakhali region of East Bengal were kidnapping Hindu women and children and forcibly converting them to Islam. He set off to tour the area and try to restore sanity. For months he walked from village to village, sharing the lives of the people and urging them to see how senseless violence was. Each day he would rise at 4 a.m. and walk several kilometres to the next village, where he would talk and pray, share a meal of fruit and vegetables with the villagers and spend the night in one of their huts. He was now seventy-six years old and this mission meant great hardship and fatigue for him.

In February 1947 a new Viceroy, Lord Mountbatten, was sent to India in an attempt to smooth negotiations. He talked patiently with Jinnah, Nehru (now prime minister) and the Mahatma. Both Mountbatten and Congress wanted a united India, but Jinnah warned that civil war would break out if the Muslims were not given a separate state. Eventually, because there seemed to be no alternative, Congress agreed to accept partition, hoping that this would at least prevent civil war.

On 15 August 1947 India and Pakistan celebrated their independence within the British Commonwealth. Mountbatten remained as Governor-General of the new Dominion of India. The Mahatma felt unable to take part in

Nehru arriving at a conference in New Delhi where India's new constitution was to be drawn up, February 1947

the celebrations, for he could see that partition was going to cause more problems than it solved.

As a result of partition millions of Hindus and Muslims became refugees, moving from one state to another. Many died in fierce clashes between the two religious groups. In Calcutta the Mahatma tried to prevent the killings. Once again he began to fast and this time hundreds of policemen and their British officers joined him in the fast, while remaining on duty.

At last he succeeded. Hindu and Muslim leaders calmed their followers and promised the Mahatma there would be no more trouble if he would end his fast. He asked them to put the promise in writing and sign it. Later, when killing was rife in the Punjab, Bengal kept its promise to him and remained calm.

The last days
In September 1947 Gandhi left for the Punjab on a mission of peace. As he began his final fast he said: "Death for me would be a deliverance rather than that I should be a helpless witness to the destruction of India." He was in great pain now. Prayers were said for him by Hindu and Muslim communities and Christian hymns were sung. Gradually the Mahatma began to recover. He seemed to have complete mastery over his body.

However, some Hindus who were angered by his defence of Muslims were plotting to kill him. They were prepared to fight to win Pakistan back for India and saw Gandhi as an obstacle in their way.

In Delhi on 30 January 1948 the Mahatma addressed a huge crowd that had gathered to hear him. Many people touched his feet as a sign of reverence.

In the crowd was a high-caste Hindu, a Brahmin, called

Godse. As he watched, Godse brooded on the atrocities he had seen inflicted on Hindus. He believed that Gandhi, because of his efforts to unite Muslims and Hindus, was responsible.

As the Mahatma lifted his arms, smiled and touched his palms together in greeting, Godse moved forward, stood in front of Gandhi and bowed. Then he fired his gun three times into Gandhi's chest. The raised arms dropped to his sides as, calling quietly to God, "He Rama", the Mahatma fell dead.

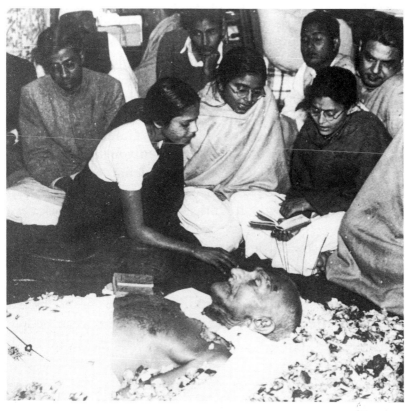

Mourners surround Gandhi's body, lying in state on banks of flower petals, shortly before his cremation

Since Gandhi

Gandhi has been called "a magnetic leader whom even his enemies could not resist" and "the most important religious figure of our time". There is a statue or picture of him in nearly every village and town in India and he is spoken of with reverence throughout the world.

Nevertheless, many of the problems Gandhi tried to solve still remain. Unemployment and over-population in India have led to terrible poverty. Few people weave their own cloth, but there has been some growth in village industries. In the early 1970s war broke out between India and Pakistan, and East Pakistan has since become an independent country, Bangladesh. Tension continues between Hindus and Muslims. India, like many other countries, now has a nuclear power industry, which Gandhi might have seen as a backward step.

No organised movement sprang from Gandhi's life, but he left as his legacy "the way of peace". Gandhi saw himself as an average man. He was sure that anyone could achieve what he achieved if they made the same effort and lived with hope and faith. He made no secret of the fact that living up to an ideal is a struggle; he himself always had to work very hard.

Gandhi once said that the crises that affect us today are not so much political as spiritual. He believed that if the lives of millions of people were rooted in the values of non-violence those values would gradually be reflected throughout the world, giving rise to peace between people and nations.

BIOGRAPHICAL NOTES

2 October 1869   Mohandas Karamchand Gandhi is born in Porbandar, India.

1882   Gandhi marries Kasturbai.

1887   Passes high-school examination.

September 1888   Sails to England to study law.

June 1891   Passes law examinations and enrols as a barrister at Inner Temple, London, returning to India shortly afterwards.

May 1893   Leaves India for Durban, South Africa.

1899–1902   Boer War.

August 1914   Outbreak of First World War.

1917   Gandhi settles dispute at Champaran, India.

1918   End of First World War.

12 August 1919   Massacre at Amritsar.

March 1922   Gandhi sentenced to six years in prison for persuading others to disobey the law.

1924   Released from prison; operation for appendicitis.

12 March–5 April 1930   The Salt March.

August 1931   Gandhi represents India at Round Table Conference in England.

20 September 1932   Fasts to improve conditions for the Harijans.

3 September 1939   Outbreak of Second World War.

1942–1944   Gandhi imprisoned in the Aga Khan's palace, Poona.

1944   Kasturbai dies.

August 1945   End of Second World War.

March 1946   British send Mission to India to prepare for handover of power.

15 August 1947   India and Pakistan celebrate independence within the British Commonwealth.

September 1947   Gandhi leaves for the Punjab on peace mission.

30 January 1948   Gandhi assassinated.

THINGS TO DO

A Test yourself

Here are some short questions. See if you can remember the answers from what you have read. Then write them down in a few words.

1 To what religion did the Gandhis belong?
2 How old was Gandhi when he married?
3 What did he study in England?
4 What is the Bhagavad-gita?
5 Why did Gandhi go to South Africa in 1893?
6 What is an ashram?
7 What did Gandhi call his weapons of peace?
8 Who were the Children of God?
9 What did Gandhi sometimes do as a last resort to make people obey him?
10 Why did Gandhi's assassin kill him?

B Think through

These questions need longer answers. Think about them, and then try to write two or three sentences in answer to each one. You may look up the story again to help you.

1 What are the main groups in the Indian caste system?
2 Describe the incident that made Gandhi decide to stay in South Africa.
3 What did he believe he must do to follow God?
4 What was Gandhi's teaching on non-violence?
5 Why did he organise the Salt March?
6 Why were the Lancashire millhands suspicious of Gandhi?
7 Ali Jinnah wanted a separate state for the Muslims. Why?
8 Why did Gandhi oppose the idea of a divided India?

C To talk about

Here are some questions for you to discuss together. Try to give reasons for what you say or think. Try to find out all the different opinions which people have about each question.

1 What do you think we can learn from Gandhi's life? Are there qualities in his character you would like to cultivate in your own?

2 Explain (a) satyagraha and (b) ahimsa. Would hartals under Gandhi's rules succeed in this country today?

3 Do you think it is possible to love your enemies and to return love for hatred? What effect do you think it would have on the other person?

4 Discuss some of the problems facing India today (including natural disasters). How do you think the West can help?

D Find out

Choose one or two of the subjects below and find out all you can about them. History books, geography books and encyclopaedias may be useful.

1 *India within the British Empire*
   (a) Draw a map of the world and colour in the countries which were in the British Empire at the turn of the century.
   (b) Write a short account of the Indian Mutiny.
   (c) Make a list of some of the ways in which India benefited under British rule.

2 *After partition*
   (a) Draw a map of India and Pakistan after partition. Mark in Porbandar, Rajkot, Ahmadabad, Punjab, Kashmir, Bengal, Calcutta, Karachi, Madras, Delhi, Noakhali, Bihar. Why do you think there have been so many clashes between Muslims and Hindus at the time of and since partition?
   (b) How has India changed since Gandhi's time? What influence, if any, does his teaching have in modern India?
   (c) Write a description of the system of government in India. Is it a democracy?

3 *Religion*
   (a) Find out something about the main religions in India and write a short account of each.
   (b) Describe life in an ashram. What do you understand by the term "meditation"?
   (c) What aspects of different religions influenced Gandhi in his search for truth?

USEFUL INFORMATION

More books to read

Amritsar – The Massacre that ended the Raj, by Alfred Draper (Cassell) (T).

Bhagavad Gita (Penguin Classics) (T).

The Bhagavad Gita for Daily Living, by Eknath Easwaran (Nilgiri Press, Petaluma, California) (T).

The British Raj and Indian Nationalism, by M. Yapp (Harrap) (P).

Books by Mahatma Gandhi:

All Men are Brothers: The Life and Thoughts of Mahatma Gandhi as Told in His Own Words (Columbia University Press, New York, and UNESCO/H.M.S.O.) (T).

Selections from Gandhi, edited by Nirmal Kumar Bose (Navajivan, Ahmadabad) (T).

The Story of My Experiments with Truth, translated by M. Desai (Penguin) (T).

Books about Mahatma Gandhi:

Gandhi, by F. W. Rawding (Cambridge Educational) (P).

Gandhi – A Life Revisited (mainly photographs) (East-West Publications) (P).

Gandhi – His Life and Message for the World, by Louis Fischer (New American Library, New York) (T).

Gandhi the Man, by Eknath Easwaran (Turnstone Press) (P/T).

Mahatma Gandhi – His Life and Influence, by Chandra Kumar and Mohinder Puri (Heinemann) (T).

(T) = suitable for teachers and older pupils
(P) = suitable for younger pupils

Films and filmstrips

Gandhi, feature film directed by Richard Attenborough, starring Ben Kingsley as Mahatma Gandhi. Available on 16 mm from Columbia-EMI-Warner, 135 Wardour Street, London W1V 4AP. Also available on video from local video shops.

Sokhodeora – The Story of an Indian Village (16 mm, 21 min), colour, and other films and filmstrips on the subject of India are available from Viewtech, 122 Goldcrest Road, Chipping Sodbury, Bristol BS17 6XN.